HOW TO FEEL

Awesome

EVERY DAY

Text copyright © 2017 by E. Bailey
Illustrations copyright © 2017 by Astred Hicks
Internal design by Astred Hicks, Design Cherry
Cover design © 2018 by Allison Sundstrom/Sourcebooks, Inc.
Image Credits © page 30 by M. K. Clinton; 76–77 by jsabirova/Shutterstock; 130–131 by
Brosko/Shutterstock; 136–137 by Denis Gorelkin/Shutterstock; 148–149 by Franzi/Shutterstock

Published by Sourcebooks Fire, an imprint of Sourcebooks, Inc.
P.O. Box 4410, Naperville, Illinois 60567-4410
(630) 961-3900
Fax: (630) 961-2168
sourcebooks.com

Originally published in 2017 in Australia by Random House Australia, an imprint of Penguin
Random House.

Library of Congress Cataloging-in-Publication Data is on file with the publisher.

Printed and bound in China.
PP 10 9 8 7 6 5 4 3 2 1

Elly Awesome

presents

HOW TO FEEL
Awesome
EVERY DAY

Illustrated by Astred Hicks

sourcebooks
fire

To my mum.
Thank you for teaching me the
importance of kindness and
understanding, and to see the
positives in all things.

Sit down and strap yourself in because I'm about to overhaul your life and turn it TOTALLY AWESOME. This book is filled with loads of pages that will kill your boredom and brighten your day. I'm talkin' journal pages, quotes, advice, DIYs, recipes, and all sorts of RAD activities.

Whether you're having some time to yourself, need some sweet ideas for hangs with friends, or the internet is down (oh, if it is, I feel for you, bro), this book is for you!

Let's be honest, we all have our own personal struggles and life isn't always easy. I mean, even **Elly Awesome** doesn't feel awesome all the time. So I've written this book to help you whenever you need to lighten the mood.

All right, are you ready to **feel awesome**?!

Then it's time to turn the page...

Elly Awesome

Pssssssst! When you see #FEELAWESOMEEVERYDAY, upload a photo and share with the HOW TO FEEL AWESOME EVERY DAY community.

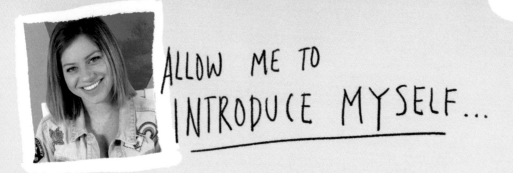

ALLOW ME TO
INTRODUCE MYSELF...

Hello there, awesome person. I'm Elly—also known as **Elly Awesome** on the interwebs—and I've been watching and uploading videos to YouTube since 2007. Since then, I've managed to turn making videos as a hobby into a full-time job, and now, about nine hundred video uploads later, it has taken over my life.

For as long as I can remember, I've been a chirpy, chubby-cheeked camera-hog, and from a young age my ultimate dream was to be a TV presenter when I grew up. My parents, although recognizing my innate nature to entertain, weren't so sure and encouraged me to follow a more "stable" career. So, I listened to their advice and I studied exercise and nutrition science, then got a degree as a dental technician. Surprise! I'm qualified to make you a set of dentures if you ever happen to need some (but please, try not to need some)!

So, there I was, lab coat on, making some of the most beautiful dentures in the land and I was having a pretty awesome time. But my childhood dream was always at the back of my mind... I still wanted to make people laugh and smile for a living. At this time the YouTuber trend was really taking off; there were so many exciting videos out there and people loved it! This was where I wanted to be and it seemed like the perfect platform to share all the funny and awesome ideas in my head. So, with YOLO as my motto, I took a step into the unknown and decided to pursue my presenting goals.

Let me tell you, chasing your dreams is HARD! I knew nothing about video production or presenting, but you gotta start somewhere, right? I began watching hundreds of tutorials online and reading books about public speaking and how to use cameras, edit videos, and make short films. I bought a camera, stuck it on a tripod, got all the lamps in the house, pointed them at my face, and started talking to the camera. And with my first video upload to my YouTube channel, Elly Awesome was born.

I took inspiration from all my favorite online creators, comedians, and filmmakers and I worked on new ideas for videos every day. I was so passionate that I used to work full-time making dentures all week and then I'd come home and make YouTube videos until the early hours of the morning. Over the years my confidence grew and I got better and better. I started to upgrade my equipment and eventually got work experience in all different places as a presenter and filmmaker.

Finally, after seven long years of hard work, sweat, and tears, I am officially able to call myself a PRESENTER.

My journey has been a whirlwind and it wouldn't have been possible without keeping my chin up, embracing hard work, and turning challenges into awesome experiences. So, when I was approached to do a book, my first thought was: WHHHAAATTTTTTTTT! Then, when I calmed down, the perfect idea popped into my head. I wanted to write a positive book to make people smile, feel happy, and help them turn daily challenges into their own awesome experiences. I have filled these pages with all the things that help me FEEL AWESOME EVERY DAY. I hope it makes you laugh, smile, and feel totally AWESOME too!

FILL THIS PAGE
WITH ALL THE THINGS
THAT MAKE YOU
FEEL AWESOME....

HOW AWESOME DO YOU FEEL RIGHT NOW?

1   5   10

COLOR
IN THE
BAR

THIS PAGE IS
ALL ABOUT YOU

SCRIBBLE DOWN SOME SUPER AWESOME
AMAZING THINGS YOU LOVE ABOUT YOURSELF

GOALS
TO ACHIEVE AWESOMENESS

So, let's get started on this road to AWESOME... What do you want to achieve this week? Next week? Next month? Or, are you planning a HUGE achievement over the next year?

Jot down your goals on this page. You have just taken your first steps on your AWESOME EVERY DAY adventure! Woo!

DAILY GOALS

GOALS FOR THE YEAR

MONTHLY GOALS

DAYS OF THE WEEK
POSITIVITY

MAKE-A-CHANGE MONDAY
It doesn't matter how small or big the gesture—a great way to start the week is to do something that will help someone else.

TRY-SOMETHING-NEW TUESDAY
Get out of your comfort zone and try something new—eat a new cuisine, try a new gym class. Whatever it is, trying something new makes you TOTALLY AWESOME.

WORK-HARD WEDNESDAY
You can't enjoy the play if you don't put in the work at some point. Today is the day to get shiz done so the rest of the week flies by and you've got more free time on the weekend. BOOM!

THUMBS-UP THURSDAY

It's nearly the weekend! Keep the positivity high and give Thursday a big THUMBS UP! Look back on the great things you've achieved this week and cross them off your to-do list.

FEEL-THE-LOVE FRIDAY

Finally, TGIF! Send your fave people a kind message today and let them know you love them.

SUPER-AWESOME SATURDAY

Oh, Saturday—I love you! Today is the day for FUN with friends and family. Why not go on a road trip or find some activity ideas in this book?

SNOOZE-TIME SUNDAY

So, you've spent the whole week being super awesome, you more than deserve a day to catch some zzzzzZZZZzzzzzs. Once you've had your chill time, get prepping for the new week! Why not make a new goals and to-do list?

Aaaannnnnnndddd REPEAT...

#SELFIE
#FEEL AWESOME EVERY DAY

HOW TO ACHIEVE
INSTANT AWESOME
~VIBES~

TALK OUT
YOUR FEELS

UNFOLLOW
PEOPLE ON
SOCIAL MEDIA
THAT GET YOU
DOWN

LIE UNDER
A TREE

DRINK SOME
TEA

WATCH A
FUNNY MOVIE

LISTEN TO
HAPPY SONGS

EAT
SOME
CAKE

GO FOR A
WALK IN
NATURE

GET CREATIVE
AND MAKE
SOMETHING

PAT A CUTE
ANIMAL OR
CUDDLE A TOY

PLAN AN
ADVENTURE

10 STAR JUMPS

10 SQUATS

10 KNEE PUSH-UPS

10 HIGH KNEES

Now, if you're still feeling up to it, do these exercises!

AWESOME MORNING EXERCISE ROUTINE

Morning, awesome people! There is no better way to start the day than with a little bit of exercise. This is my super-easy morning workout. If you're not feeling very motivated, set a five-minute timer and do these exercises until the alarm goes off. Even after just one set, you'll feel totally energized and ready to take on the day! Come on now, drag that lazy butt out of bed and LET'S GO!

$$\frac{10}{\text{SIT-UPS}}$$

$$\frac{10}{\text{LUNGES}}$$

$$\frac{20}{\text{STAR JUMPS}}$$

awesome overnight oats

Are you one of those peeps who skips brekkie in the morning? If you are, tell me, how UN-AWESOME do you feel by about 10 a.m.? Let me guess, you're still half asleep, you feel like the grumpiest person in the room, and your stomach sounds like it has an angry monster living inside it. Wait, what was that you just said? "Miss Awesome, how did you know?!" Well, awesome people, listen up, *BREAKFAST IS THE MOST IMPORTANT MEAL OF THE DAY.* It's not rocket science! When you wake up from a big night of snoring, your energy stores are low. You're like a car with no gas in the tank...pretty useless! So, to enable your brain and muscles to work, you have to "break the fast," fill up your tank, and get the day off to an AWESOME start.

If you're anything like me, I'm always in a rush in the morning, so these overnight oats are my all-time favorite, time-saving breakfast. I make a batch the night before so the creamy deliciousness is just waiting in the fridge, ready for me to grab in the morning. YUM!

INGREDIENTS

⅓ cup rolled oats
(avoid steel-cut oats as they
stay crunchy, and instant/
quick oats turn too gummy)

⅓ cup milk
(use a plant-based milk to
make this recipe vegan)

⅔ cup plain Greek yogurt

2 tablespoons honey
(golden syrup or maple syrup
to be vegan)

OPTIONAL

½ teaspoon vanilla extract
(extra tasty vanilla flavor)

SIMPLE OVERNIGHT OATS (base recipe)

🗲 For this recipe you will need to use a
jar or container that seals with a tight-
fitting lid.

🗲 Add all the ingredients to your jar
or container and mix together. Once
combined, seal the jar and place in the
fridge overnight.

🗲 If you really want to eat these sooner,
they will be good to go after about
4 hours.

MAKES 1 SERVING

AWESOME TIP ALERT

ADD YOUR FAVE CHOPPED
NUTS OR GRANOLA ON TOP
FOR EXTRA AWESOMENESS!

Pssst, awesome people, this is the fun part...now
you've got the basic recipe mastered, let's mix it up
and try out these AMAZINGLY AWESOME variations!
Follow the recipe above and simply add these delicious
ingredients before leaving in the fridge overnight.

FOR CHOC-PEANUT OVERNIGHT OATS

2 tablespoons of cocoa powder

2 tablespoons of unsweetened natural
peanut butter

FOR APPLE CINNAMON OVERNIGHT OATS

¼–½ teaspoon cinnamon

⅓ cup apple pieces, finely chopped

FOR COCONUT STRAWBERRY OVERNIGHT OATS

¼ cup of fresh strawberries, chopped

¼ cup of coconut flakes

If you want a more intense coconut
flavor, use coconut milk instead
of regular milk

Add more of your own ideas. We want that
BIG heart overflowing with
AWESOME FEELS!

WRITE A FRIEND
A POSITIVE NOTE

CALL A LOVED
ONE YOU
HAVEN'T SPOKEN
TO IN A WHILE

Make someone
an awesome playlist

CLEAN THE
HOUSE FOR
YOUR MUM
& DAD~

VOLUNTEER
FOR CHARITY

Help a friend
who is having
a hard time

HOW TO MAKE
SOMEONE ELSE FEEL
AWESOME

MAKE DINNER
FOR YOUR
FAM

Be a shoulder
to cry on

GIVE YOUR
LOVED ONES
A BIG
HUG

KINDNESS,

like a boomerang,

ALWAYS

RETURNS

JAR OF HAPPINESS

Get a jar and label it "HAPPINESS." Your mission is to fill your jar with 365 days of awesome. Each day, if something AWESOME happens, write it down on a small piece of paper, fold it up and pop it in the jar.

Obviously, awesome might not happen every day, so on these days take some time to reflect on what you are grateful for or the super-awesome people (or animals) in your life who make you happy.

The coolest part of your jar of happiness is being able to open it at any time, pull out a note and remember all the awesome times you've had.

~~ONE DAY~~ I WILL

I think challenging yourself is pretty awesome. It's a great way to build confidence and grow. And, more often than not, you totally surprise yourself with what you can accomplish when you put your mind to it. So, awesome people, this page is all about new challenges. Whether it's a fitness challenge or a more personal challenge like overcoming a fear, write it down and set a deadline to work towards. Remember, the most important thing when it comes to challenges is making a start. Even if you don't quite achieve what you set out to do in the beginning, it's all about trying your best. I guarantee when that date comes around, you will feel proud and pretty awesome.

~~ONE DAY~~ I WILL

_____

_____

_____

_____

_____

Deadline _____

Signed   _____

DEAR SELF
YOU CAN
DO THIS.
MAKE IT
HAPPEN.
YOU ARE
AWESOME

ALL MY
LOVE,
ME

awesome energy bites

So, I admit, I'm a snacker. To get me through the day and keep my energy levels up (and the HANGER at bay) I have to have my snacks. HOWEVER, chips, dips and chocolates are not what you're going to find here, sorry to disappoint. To enable SUPER-PRODUCTIVE AWESOMENESS in the classroom or at work, we have to be healthy.

These no-bake chewy treats are healthy, delicious, and easy to make. Also, speaking from personal experience, they pretty much make you feel like an unstoppable superhero!

So, to all the other snackers out there, step away from the chocolate, this recipe is for you.

INGREDIENTS

2 cups walnuts
  (or your favorite nuts)

1/2 cup shredded coconut,
  unsweetened

2 cups pitted Medjool dates

2 tablespoons coconut oil

½ teaspoon sea salt

1 teaspoon vanilla extract

*
ADDED BONUS
ALL THE
INGREDIENTS ARE
VEGAN FRIENDLY
*

AWESOME ENERGY BITES

✎ With a food processor, whiz up the walnuts and shredded coconut until broken down and crumbly.

✎ Add the remaining ingredients and blend for about a minute until combined. The mixture should become sticky.

✎ Use your (clean) hands to roll the mixture into little balls. Place them on a plate and leave in the fridge for an hour. DONE!

You can eat these AWESOME ENERGY BITES straight away, cold or frozen. They will last for almost a week in a sealed container, but they will last longer if you freeze them.

MAKES 15–20 BALLS, DEPENDING ON SIZE

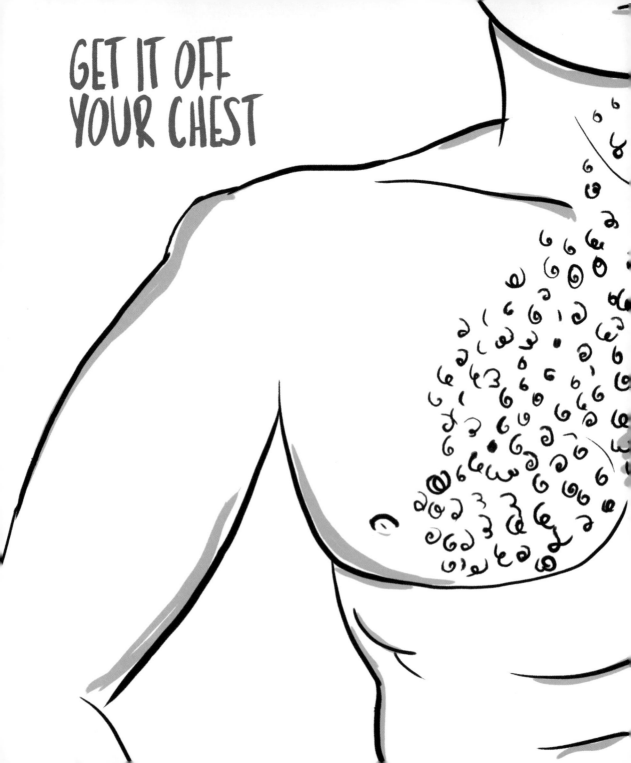

Feeling frustrated? Take it out on this page...
Write down all the things that are really ticking you
off! I guarantee you will feel AWESOME
after you've let them out.

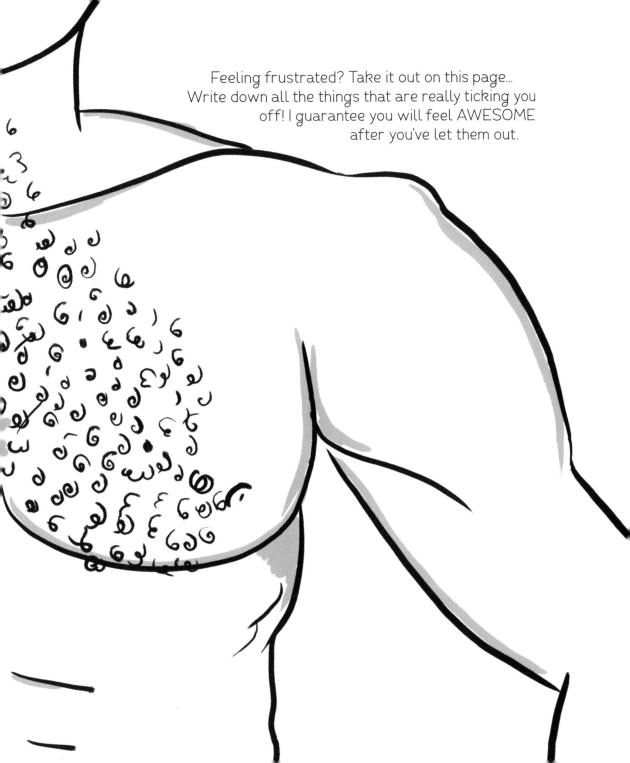

the UNDO LIST

I love a to-do list as much as the next super-organized geek (FYI being a geek is totally cool). But the other day, an awesome thought suddenly came to me—instead of writing lists about what we have TO DO, why don't we flip it and make a list of all the things we've got TO STOP DOING. Working out the things you need to stop doing can be just as effective to your productivity as working out what you've got to do.

So, awesome people, introducing...
THE UNDO LIST!

Use this page to scribble down all the things you need to stop doing (cut out the hours of social media time...nudge, nudge) so you can be more productive.

PERFECT YOUR
SUPER-AWESOME
AMAZING
signature
HERE

Practice on this page until it's full!

Smile today

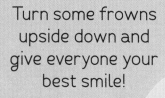

Turn some frowns upside down and give everyone your best smile!

← DRAW YOUR BEST FUNNY FACES ↑ ↓ ←

THE WORLD
WOULD BE A
NICER
PLACE
IF EVERYONE
HAD THE ABILITY
TO LOVE
AS UNCONDITIONALLY AS
A DOG
M·K·
CLINTON

WHAT I LEARNED FROM MY DOG

Every day is a new and exciting day. Smell everything. Everything smells good (apparently).

Digging in the garden can be very therapeutic.

Greet people like you haven't seen them for years and you'll fill them with joy.

Exercise makes you feel good. At least one walk a day will help you feel happier and more content.

Food is awesome. Enjoy each meal like you haven't eaten in days. Don't take it for granted.

Be loyal to those who are kind and respectful to you.

AWESOME IDEAS
for bored bodies

Make up a super-awesome
dance routine

Try to balance ten marshmallows
on your face and head

Plan a day of fun with your bestie

Make a chatterbox (see page 104)

Attempt to juggle some fruit or vegetables

Only use your less dominant hand for
the rest of the day

Use chalk to draw a masterpiece on
your footpath or driveway

Try to touch your nose with your elbow
(good luck – this is usually impossible)

Make a fort out of sofa cushions

Make Oobleck (see page 98)

Make up a secret handshake

THERE'S NO
TIME
TO BE
BORED.

I'M TOO BUSY
BEING
AWESOME!

WATCH THE CLOUDS GO BY. . .

I think clouds are AWESOME. They are so calming and I love the shapes, patterns, and colors they make in the sky. Also, they aren't just floaty, fluffy things, they are so much more! Seriously, google it. SO, we should all take some time out from the daily grind and enjoy some cloud time—it will clear your mind!

There is one rule for cloud time and ONE rule only—NO PHONES!!! How can anyone get ZEN with a phone pinging and buzzing nonstop?

CLOUD TIME TIPS

1. GRAB A BLANKET OR TOWEL

2. PICK A QUIET SPOT—PARK, BEACH, BACKYARD—I WOULD ADVISE AGAINST A BUSY AREA

3. PUT A PILLOW UNDER YOUR NECK FOR ULTIMATE COMFORT

4. LIE DOWN AND LET YOUR IMAGINATION RUN WILD! SEE IF YOU CAN SPOT ANYTHING COOL AND WEIRD—SOMETIMES CLOUDS LOOK LIKE CRAZY CREATURES OR PEOPLE'S FACES

5. CLOUD TIME IS ALSO GREAT WITH A BUNCH OF FRIENDS

What are you waiting for?! Get your butts outside and get looking at that beautiful sky. Trust me, after this, you will feel super chill and super awesome!

*

FOR BONUS AWESOMENESS, BRING SOME ICE CREAMS AND SNACKS ALONG

*

A LITTLE BOX OF
AWESOMENESS

Nothing says awesome like
a homemade gift, so why not
surprise someone? Trust me,
these little gift boxes are
serious friend-pleasers and
they're so easy to make!

Cut out the template and transfer it onto some
sturdy card. If you want to make a bigger box,
photocopy the template and
increase the size. You can
decorate the card with your
own designs or you can use
some snazzy wrapping paper.
Glue the tabs where instructed
and VOILÀ! A little box of
awesomeness.

Once you've made the box, fill it with an awesome
surprise—maybe some chocolates, a little
keepsake, a picture, or even a simple note
(you can get help with that from page 87).

GLUE THE BACK
OF THIS FLAP

GLUE THE BACK
OF THIS FLAP

GLUE THE BACK
OF THIS FLAP

GLUE THE BACK
OF THIS FLAP

cut ——————

fold ••••••••••••

WHAT KIND OF SHORTS DO CLOUDS WEAR?

THUNDERWEAR

AWESOME THINGS TO DO ON A RAINY DAY

CHECK LIST

- ○ Bake something
- ○ Read a book
- ○ Make an indoor fort
- ○ Throw a DANCE PARTY
- ○ Paint a masterpiece
- ○ Play hide-and-seek
- ○ Take a bath
- ○ Listen to music

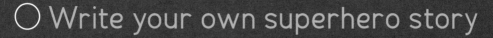
○ Write your own superhero story

○ Have a tea party

○ Create a collage of your favorite pics

○ Play indoor volleyball with a balloon

○ Make paper airplanes until you make one that flies really far!

○ Make your own music video

○ Learn to moonwalk

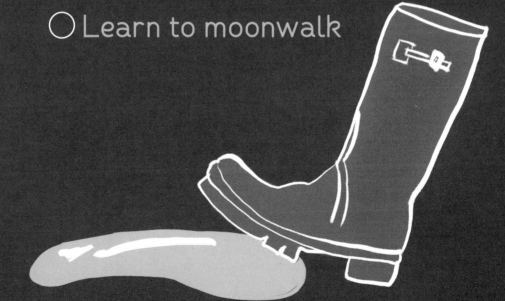

mega-awesome choc-chip mug cake

Ever baked a cake and thought, "Wow, that's just so much cake. I don't think I can eat it all! I sure wish I hadn't made so much..."? Yeah, me neither. Cake is amazing. I love cake! But I guess it does take a little while to prepare and bake. So, what do you do when you've got those cake cravings? Well, what if you could whip up a single serving of cake in just two minutes? Yep, it's possible. I know—I'm amazing.

Here is my fave mug cake recipe. What are mug cakes exactly? They are single-serve cakes that you can make in a mug and cook in your microwave! Not only is it quick, but I also made this recipe really easy. In fact, you only need a mug, a spoon, and the ingredients. No measuring cups, no weighing, no...wait, you're still reading this? Dude, how are you not making this already? Get going!

INGREDIENTS

1 tablespoon butter

1 tablespoon white sugar

1 tablespoon brown sugar

3 drops vanilla extract

1 pinch salt

1 egg yolk

3 tablespoons self-rising flour

2 tablespoons chocolate chips

MEGA-AWESOME
CHOC-CHIP MUG CAKE

- Spoon the butter into your microwave-safe mug and place in the microwave for 10 seconds on high.
- Add the white and brown sugar, vanilla and salt to the melted butter. MIX.
- Separate your egg; add the yolk to the your mug and discard the white. (Or save for an egg white omelet tomorrow morning!) MIX.
- Add the flour. MIX.
- Place your mug back in the microwave and cook on high for 40 seconds. If after 40 seconds the cake seems too moist, microwave on high for a further 10–20 seconds.

MAKES 1 SERVING

HOW TO STOP PROCRASTINATING

Let's be honest, we are all guilty of pretending to work when you are actually 52 weeks deep in someone's Instagram page. This, my friend, is not awesome. That cute puppy meme you've been watching over and over for the last hour is not going to do your assignment for you!

THINGS I DO WHEN I REALLY NEED TO GET SOME IMPORTANT WORK DONE:

TELL PEOPLE I HAVE TO GET REALLY IMPORTANT WORK DONE

DO MY IMPORTANT WORK

HERE'S HOW TO AVOID GETTING SUCKED INTO THE PROCRASTINATION VOID

☺ Don't work in your pajamas

☺ Make a to-do list and cross it off as you go

☺ Give yourself a set amount of time for "free-time fun" where you can relax and socialize

☺ Take breaks by going for walks in the fresh air

☺ Do your work in different environments

FEELING STUCK?

Deadlines are looming and you just can't get started. *ARRRGGGHHHH!* This is what you've got to do. Set a timer for five minutes and decide to dedicate yourself COMPLETELY to doing your work (even if you are just putting together a mega-awesome to-do list). See how much you can get done in those five minutes and then increase the time period and do it again (and repeat). You'll be surprised by how this helps to kick-start your brain and get things rolling!

RANDOM ACTS OF
KINDNESS

We can never know exactly what is going on in other people's lives—this applies to our friends and family as well as strangers we walk past every day. What if someone is having a blue day? Wouldn't it be awesome to make their day that bit better by a random act of kindness? It won't just make them feel awesome—you'll feel awesome too! Below are some simple things you can do for others.

Let someone go ahead of you in a line

Take a friend out for coffee and cake

Hold a door open for someone

Smile at someone

Give someone a genuine compliment

Give someone a handmade gift

Run an errand for someone

Cook someone dinner

Help someone carry their bags

Donate your old clothes to charity

TIME to TEAR IT UP

TAKE WHAT YOU NEED

TEAR HERE

HAPPINESS
IS KNOWING THAT
IN A
PARALLEL
UNIVERSE,
MOST LIKELY,
YOU'RE A
SUPERHERO

-ANONYMOUS

ELLY AWESOME AND LI'L BEAN

Some of you might not know that I, Elly Awesome, am in fact a legit superhero...for reals. HA, I almost had you there, didn't I? Sadly, I am not, BUT that doesn't stop me dreaming. You never know, one day you might get bitten by that spider and BOOM. You're a superhero.

Here's how I see myself as a superhero, along with my super-cute doggy sidekick, Li'l Bean!

LI'L BEAN

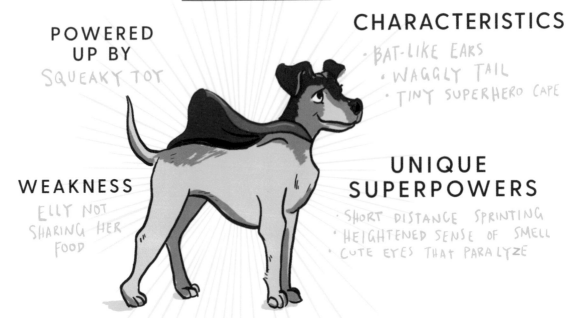

POWERED UP BY
SQUEAKY TOY

CHARACTERISTICS
- BAT-LIKE EARS
- WAGGLY TAIL
- TINY SUPERHERO CAPE

WEAKNESS
ELLY NOT SHARING HER FOOD

UNIQUE SUPERPOWERS
- SHORT DISTANCE SPRINTING
- HEIGHTENED SENSE OF SMELL
- CUTE EYES THAT PARALYZE

ELLY AWESOME

UNIQUE SUPERPOWERS
- BOTTOMLESS PIT OF A STOMACH
- NINJA-LIKE STEALTH AND AGILITY
- CAN TALK PEOPLE TO SLEEP

POWERED UP BY
PIZZA

CHARACTERISTICS
- MUSCULAR
- CHARMING CHUBBY CHEEKS
- DAZZLING BLUE EYES

WEAKNESS
HUNGER

IF YOU WERE A SUPERHERO, WHAT WOULD YOUR POWERS BE?

_____

_____

_____

HOW DID YOU BECOME A SUPERHERO?

_____

_____

_____

WHAT WOULD YOUR SUPERHERO NAME BE?

_____

_____

_____

DO YOU HAVE AN AWESOME SIDEKICK?

_____

_____

_____

WHO IS YOUR ULTIMATE NEMESIS?

_____

_____

_____

USE THE TEMPLATE OPPOSITE TO DRAW YOUR SUPERHERO!
AS YOU ADD CLOTHES, YOU CAN CHANGE THE BODY SHAPE OF YOUR SUPERHERO.

HERO NAME

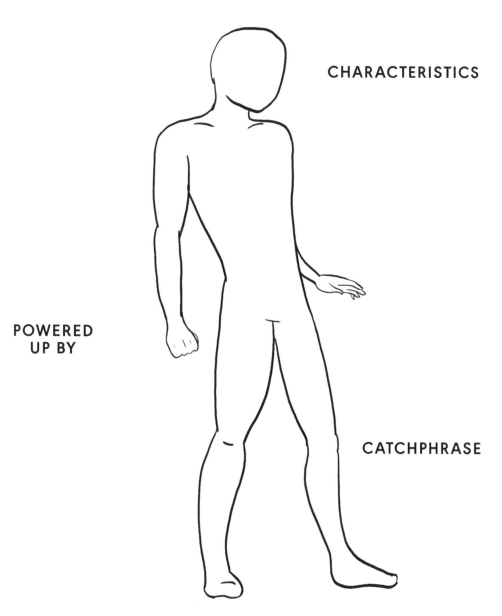

CHARACTERISTICS

POWERED
UP BY

CATCHPHRASE

THE END

SUMMER BUCKET LIST

It's SUMMER! Go forth and BE AWESOME!!!

- ○ Make a kite
- CHECK LIST → ○ Organize a picnic party
- ○ Watch the sunrise
- ○ Make your own short film
- ○ Make Oobleck (see page 98)
- ○ Watch the sunset
- ○ Make a super-awesome summer playlist

56

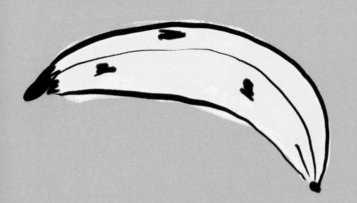

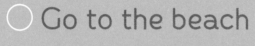

○ Go to the beach

○ Bake a cake

○ Make a Slip 'N Slide

○ Have breakfast for dinner

○ Read an awesome new book

○ Plant a tree

○ Dig the biggest hole EVER
on the beach

○ Make a WATERMELON FROSTY
(see next page)

Watermelon Frosty

Picture the scene...it's a Saturday and the sun is SHINING. You're by the pool getting your tan on and flicking through your amazing new book *How to Feel Awesome Every Day*. I know, how could this day get any better? But then, you're handed a glass full of this heavenly nectar. You think to yourself, *What is this fresh, frosty, fruity glass of deliciousness?*

Well, my friend, it is my awesome summer thirst-quencher, the Watermelon Frosty.

INGREDIENTS

WATERMELON FROSTY

2 cups watermelon, cut into
  cubes, frozen

1 banana, cut into coins, frozen

1 tablespoon honey
  (or maple syrup)

Juice of one lemon

½ cup water

✎ Cut up the watermelon and banana,
  then freeze for 4 hours or overnight.

✎ When you are ready to make your
  frosty, remove the watermelon and
  banana from the freezer and defrost for
  10 minutes.

✎ Place the watermelon and banana in a
  blender and add the honey, lemon juice
  and water.

✎ Blend all the ingredients together, pour
  into glasses and serve.

SERVES 2 PEOPLE

LET'S GO FLY A KITE!

Now, awesome people, on this road to FEELING AWESOME EVERY DAY, I think it's important to let go and embrace your inner kid once in a while. There is no better way to do this than flying a kite! So, forget about that assignment for a few hours and take a time-out. Getting outside, looking up at the sky, running around like no one's watching and flying a kite is so chill... I totally recommend it!

If you don't own a kite, don't panic! Here are some simple instructions to make your own, one-of-a-kind kite. YOU. ARE. WELCOME.

YOU WILL NEED

★ Paper with AWESOME pattern: wrapping paper, regular paper, or newspaper

★ 2 wooden dowels or very straight, lightweight sticks from the garden (one 24 in., one 20 in.)

★ String

★ Scissors

★ Tape

★ Ribbons

INSTRUCTIONS

1. Using something sharp, carefully cut notches into the ends of your dowels/ sticks.

2. Place the smaller stick on top of the larger stick (about 6 in. from the top of the larger stick) and wrap string around them in a crisscross pattern to tie them together.

3. Wrap string around the whole kite frame, making sure the string is tightly secured through all four notches in the ends of the dowels. Tie string with a secure knot.

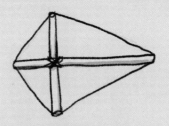

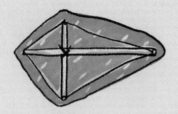

4. Lay the kite frame on top of your jazzy paper. Cut out your kite, leaving an extra 2 in. of paper around the frame.

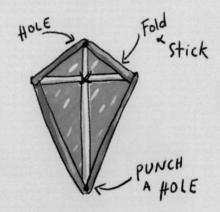

HOLE

Fold & Stick

PUNCH A HOLE

5. Fold the extra paper over the string frame and stick down with tape. Double up with more tape on all corners to make sure it's super secure.

6. Punch a hole into the top and the bottom of your kite.

7. Cut a piece of string 24 in. long (the length of your kite). Tie the string through the punched holes, top to bottom and secure with more tape.

8. Now it's time to add your flying string. You might need to adjust the position of your flying string when you first take out your kite, but I found tying it about 1/3 of the way down worked really well.

9. Attach an awesome tail with cool decorations.

ALL DONE! NOW GET OUTSIDE AND FLY A KITE!

Funky Fruit pops

These are my three favorite popsicle recipes. You'll be surprised at just how AWESOME they are for a homemade treat! Like, who needs to BUY popsicles? Psh! You'll never need to leave the house again!

INGREDIENTS

1 cup frozen strawberries

1 cup plain vanilla yogurt

STRAWBERRY YOGURT POPS

- Puree the strawberries and then mix together with the yogurt.
- Fill up popsicle molds and freeze for 3 hours or until solid.

MAKES APPROX. 6-8 POPS

INGREDIENTS

4 cups frozen pineapple

1 cup coconut milk

2 teaspoons vanilla extract

PINEAPPLE COCONUT POPS

- ✗ Using a food processor, blend all the ingredients together until it turns into a smooth mixture.
- ✗ Pour into popsicle molds and freeze for about 3 hours or until solid.

MAKES APPROX. 10 POPS

*

AWESOME TIP ALERT

IF YOU DON'T OWN POPSICLE MOLDS, YOU CAN USE PAPER OR PLASTIC CUPS AND WOODEN STICKS.

*

INGREDIENTS

2 cups boiling water

2 tea bags

1 tablespoon lemon juice (or about half the juice of one lemon)

3 tablespoons white sugar

LEMON ICE TEA POPS

- ✗ Pour the boiling water into a bowl or a big cup and steep your tea bags in it for 10 minutes.
- ✗ Once the tea has infused, remove the bags and add the lemon juice.
- ✗ Add the sugar, then stir until most of the sugar has dissolved.
- ✗ Pour into popsicle molds and freeze for 3 hours or until solid.

MAKES APPROX. 4–8 POPS

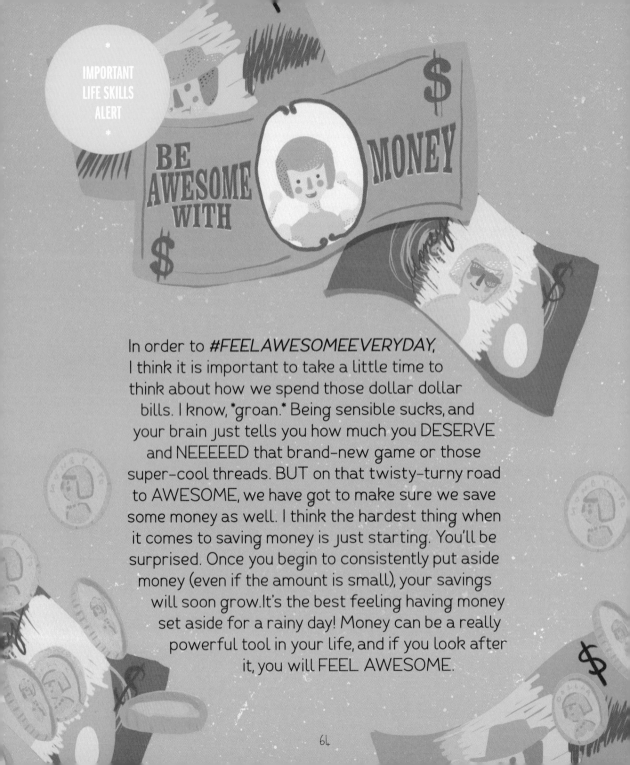

BE
AWESOME
WITH
MONEY
$

In order to *#FEELAWESOMEEVERYDAY*,
I think it is important to take a little time to
think about how we spend those dollar dollar
bills. I know, *groan.* Being sensible sucks, and
your brain just tells you how much you DESERVE
and NEEEEED that brand-new game or those
super-cool threads. BUT on that twisty-turny road
to AWESOME, we have got to make sure we save
some money as well. I think the hardest thing when
it comes to saving money is just starting. You'll be
surprised. Once you begin to consistently put aside
money (even if the amount is small), your savings
will soon grow. It's the best feeling having money
set aside for a rainy day! Money can be a really
powerful tool in your life, and if you look after
it, you will FEEL AWESOME.

HERE ARE MY SUPER-SAVER TIPS TO GET YOU STARTED!

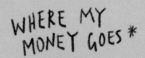

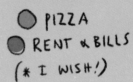

💰 Whenever you get money, no matter how small the amount, always put some of it aside into a piggy bank or bank account.

💰 Don't buy anything you can't afford (don't go into debt whenever possible).

💰 If you want to buy something expensive, wait a few weeks and then decide if you still want to buy it.

💰 If you can't afford two of the item, consider whether you can really afford it at all.

💰 Have a bank account dedicated to saving money, where you don't take money out unless it's for an emergency (and no, a "fashion emergency" doesn't count).

💰 Don't buy bottled water (if you can avoid it). Always pack your own.

💰 Make lunches in bulk instead of buying them.

💰 Make cards and gifts for your friends and family members instead of buying them.

💰 Shop at thrift stores.

💰 Look out for free events and activities in your hometown to save money on fun times.

#FEELAWESOMEEVERYDAY
TIPS FOR :SUCCESS:

Do you ever have those daydreams where you are a SUPER-AWESOME SUCCESS at all and everything you do? Yeah, me too. Whether you are at school or starting your first job, take a look at these tips and give them a go!

☺ Set dates to accomplish goals

☺ Make to-do (or undo) lists

☺ Network

☺ Always be open to learning new skills

☺ Be open-minded and calm

☺ Practice

☺ Know that it will take time (maybe even years!)

☺ Believe in yourself (sometimes you're the only one that believes in you and that's OK)

☺ Take time out to have fun

☺ Learn from your mistakes—what can you improve on next time?

☺ Don't be afraid to ask for help

☺ Put up a big wall calendar and mark down all your important deadlines and tasks

☺ Take on challenges

☺ Try to make a regular study time when you sit down and get work done

☺ Focus on accomplishing one task at a time (try not to use your phone while working!)

☺ Try writing notes by hand instead of using a computer

☺ DREAM BIG!

☺ Embrace the UNDO list!

YOU'LL BE A SUPER SUCCESS IN NO TIME!

TOUGH CALL WORKSHEET

Is your brain shutting down? Are you stuck because you've got to make a really tough call and can't work out what to do? Well, don't feel stressed, it's just time to work things out!

This super-awesome worksheet will help you break things down so you can figure out how you're feeling and how to move forward.

Decision needed by

_____

Best-case scenario

_____

_____

_____

Worst-case scenario

_____

_____

_____

Gut feelings

_____

_____

_____

Decision

_____

_____

_____

Next steps

_____

_____

_____

#FEELAWESOMEEVERYDAY

Fill this page with some of
your favorite awesome photos!

FEELING SAD?

LET'S WORK THROUGH THIS

Awesome people, as you know, this wonderful book is called *How to Feel Awesome Every Day*. The "How to" part of the title is a little giveaway here. Obviously, you're not going to be feeling awesome EVERY SINGLE DAY. Every now and then when life gets us down, we need a little guidance to get us back on track. So, when you have those weepy days and all you want to do is curl up into a ball and hide under your covers, take this book with you and we can work through it together.

If you don't want to talk out your feels with a friend, the next best thing is writing it all down. So, I created this questionnaire to help you work through the sads. Give it a go and good luck, awesome person. I know you'll get through it!

Write down how you're feeling now.

_____

_____

Why do you feel this way?

_____

_____

Will it still be a big deal next week?

_____

_____

Is there anything you can change or do to make things better?

_____

_____

What would help you feel better?

_____

_____

Is there someone you can talk to?

_____

_____

Write down your reflections and thoughts after a good night's sleep.

_____

_____

_____

Ridiculously Rad Rice Bar treats

Oh man, do I even need to explain what this recipe is? It's all in the title! These rice bar treats are RAD! If you feel like impressing your friends, then whip up this recipe real quick! Everyone will be wanting one. They're like a party for your mouth and they're a really fun lunch-box treat.

INGREDIENTS

3 tablespoons butter

4 cups mini marshmallows

5 cups crisp rice cereal

RIDICULOUSLY RAD RICE BAR TREATS

↗ In a microwave-safe container, heat the butter and marshmallows for 2 minutes on high.

↗ Remove from the microwave and give the mixture a stir. Place back in the microwave for 30 seconds until the mixture has completely melted and has turned into a smooth paste.

↗ Add the cereal to the marshmallow mixture and fold in the until completely covered.

↗ Spoon the mixture onto a baking tray lined with baking paper. Spread the mixture out so it fills the tin.

↗ Place in the freezer for 2 hours, then cut it into bars and eat. NOM!

These rad little treats can be stored in the fridge or freezer for a few days.

MAKES APPROX. 20 BARS

PAPER FLOWER DIY

Hands up: who LOVES being sent flowers? Yep, I thought
so. It's the best! Flowers are awesome—all the colors,
all the smells...only downside, they never last that long.
CRY Well, awesome people, have I got the DIY project
for you! These paper flowers look SO cool, they are
super easy to make AND they will last FOREVER!
A bouquet of these babies would make a brilliant
birthday present, a marvelous gift for your mum, or a
sweet surprise for your second cousin! So, be awesome
and make someone's day.

YOU WILL NEED

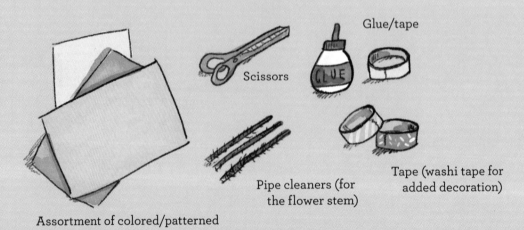

Scissors

Glue/tape

Pipe cleaners (for
the flower stem)

Tape (washi tape for
added decoration)

Assortment of colored/patterned
letter paper or card

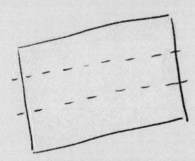

1. Get a piece of paper/card and cut it into 3 strips.

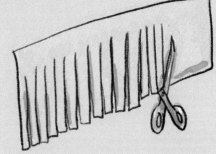

2. Take each strip and, leaving a ½ in. margin along the length of one edge, cut a "fringe." These will form the flower petals.

3. Tightly roll up the strip and secure in place with tape or glue.

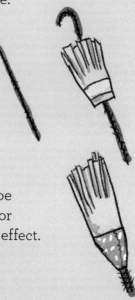

4. Using a pipe cleaner for the flower's stem, make a tiny hook on one end and feed it down the top of your flower so it hooks in.

5. When you have the stem in place, wrap tape around the base of the flower. Try colored or patterned washi tape for a super-awesome effect.

6. Now fold open the paper "petals."

DONE!

7. Repeat steps 1–6 and keep making these flowers until you have a whole bunch!

#DOSOMETHINGAWESOME

VOLUNTEER

Helping people can make you feel awesome!

Many studies have shown that helping other people improves *your* happiness. Volunteering can also help reduce stress, combat depression, and improve your self-esteem and confidence! So, no-brainer, right? Let's get out there and *#DOSOMETHINGAWESOME*!

Why volunteer?

☺ To help other people

☺ To meet new people

☺ To learn new skills

☺ To try new careers

☺ To get involved in your local community

☺ To make new friends

☺ To improve your confidence

☺ To improve your communication skills

☺ To make a difference

☺ To feel happier

Where to volunteer?

Get in touch with any of the following places and offer your time.

☺ Local charities
☺ Nursing homes
☺ Schools
☺ Local events

☺ Hospitals
☺ Your friends, family and neighbours
☺ Emergency services

Sometimes people need help with things as simple as:

☺ Cleaning
☺ Filing
☺ Cooking
☺ Planting trees
☺ Event organization
☺ Dog walking

☺ Babysitting
☺ Fundraising
☺ Data entry
☺ Tutoring
☺ Grocery shopping

There are so many ways to help people and the community!
Get creative!

#BESTIE   #SELFIE
#BFF   #FEEL AWESOME EVERY DAY

IF YOU
HAVE A
BEST
FRIEND
AS
~WEIRD~
AS YOU ←
YOU HAVE
EVERYTHING

Trading Card
D.I.Y.

Trading cards are so fun to collect and trade! But isn't it cool when you own ultra-rare ones? Well, if you make them yourself, they'll be one-of-a-kind originals. Here's your chance to get super creative and make something totally limited edish!

Design and cut out your own trading cards here. Encourage your friends to do the same! See who can make the most colorful, cool-looking cards and then trade them! Maybe you can even create your own game with them...

Sometimes it's hard to show your bestie and loved ones just how much you appreciate them. So, why not write them a letter?

DEAR _____

I'M WRITING YOU THIS NOTE BECAUSE I THINK YOU ARE _____

AND MAYBE I DON'T TELL YOU ENOUGH.
YOU ALWAYS MAKE ME FEEL _____

AND I REALLY LIKE _____

FROM _____

As the newly appointed president of the
AWESOME EVERY DAY APPRECIATION SOCIETY,
it is your job to promote the *HOW TO FEEL AWESOME*
message to the people. Design some super-awesome
badges to help spread the word!

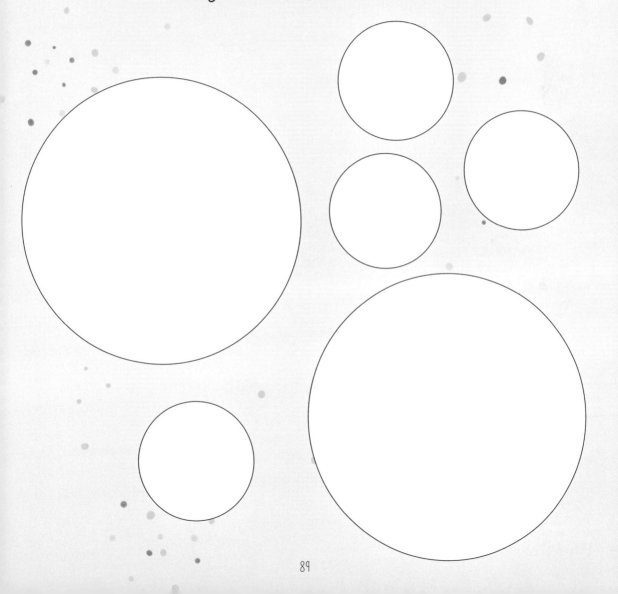

CHILL OUT

We all have those times when we fall off the AWESOME wagon and need some TLC. There is no denying life can be pretty exhausting, physically AND mentally. So, it's super important to nurture our inner awesome and get back on track. Here are a few tips!

FOR PHYSICAL AWESOMENESS

Get a massage

Bathe in Epsom salt

Take a nap

Drink plenty of water

Make healthier food choices

Go for regular walks

Get enough sleep to feel refreshed

Stretch

FOR MENTAL
AWESOMENESS

Open up to someone

Write down how you feel

Watch a funny video or movie

Take time out for yourself

Take breaks from social media

Read books that interest you
or teach you skills

Congratulate yourself on
your successes

Enjoy the sunshine

Get Zen

WITH A MINIATURE DESKTOP GARDEN

I am all about making my workspace super ZEN. Think about it. If you create a chaos-free desk space when you are studying for exams or finishing those overdue assignments, you will be way more focused. So, to help channel your inner chill, let's talk about ZEN GARDENS.

These awesome little desktop delights use rocks, sand and gravel to recreate the essence of nature. They originated in Japan and are more commonly known as Japanese rock gardens or *karesansui*, which means "dry landscape." The raking and the maintenance of the Zen garden helps you meditate and reflect on life. There is no right or wrong way to maintain a Zen garden and they are totally awesome for de-stressing, so let's get to making one!

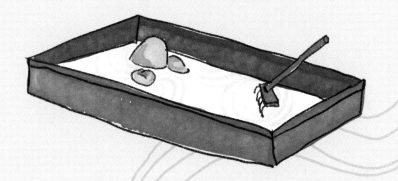

All you need is an empty container or a frame.
Then gather some sand, unique rocks (smooth ones
look awesome), seashells, sticks, and tiny plants from
outside. Fill your container with sand, smooth it out,
and place your rocks and other items in it. The order
and pattern is up to you. Use a fork to rake different
patterns in the sand. You should rearrange the items
and rake the sand whenever you want to de-stress.

SCAVENGER HUNT

I love going on long walks through my neighborhood. Walking is a great way to get energized and keep fit without much effort. It's fun to see the different styles and colors of houses in the area and maybe meet a cat roaming around or a dog behind a fence. But it's also pretty easy to be comfy at home, just chillin' on my phone. To get myself motivated and out walking, I often turn my walks into scavenger hunts. What's a scavenger hunt you say? It's where you go out adventuring and track down items that are on a list. I've created an AWESOME one for you to try here!

Put on a hat, sunglasses, and sunscreen if need be. Pack a backpack with some yummy snacks, a water bottle, and a pen, and jot down the items opposite on a scrap of paper. Your mission is to try to find everything on the list around your neighborhood. Check the items off as you find them. Scavenger hunts are awesome to do with your friends— you can even compete to be the first person to find every item (or the most items) on the list!

*

SAFETY ALERT
REMEMBER TO STAY SAFE! DON'T VENTURE TOO FAR FROM HOME AND STICK WITH YOUR FRIENDS.

*

- AN ORANGE LEAF
- A SPARKLY OR SHINY ROCK
- A FEATHER
- SOMETHING HEART-SHAPED
- A SMOOTH ROCK
- A FLOWER
- A STICK THAT LOOKS LIKE THE LETTER "Y"
- A SEED / SEED POD
- FOOTPRINTS OR ANIMAL PRINTS
- A WATER DROPLET
- AN UNUSUAL GATE
- SOMETHING TWISTY / BENDY
- A NUT

FIND ANY UNUSUAL ITEMS ON YOUR ADVENTURE?

_____

Salad Jars

Why cram a salad into a jar you say? Good question! Surely it didn't just take off because it looks good in an Instagram photo? Well, let me break it down for you—it's a good way to transport your salad, practice portion control, have the salad all ready to go, and it takes up less room in your bag. And, let's face it, they do look pretty cool.

Here are some of my fave salad jar recipes that will fill you up and have you lookin' like a cool kid at lunch.

Stack up those ingredients!

SALAD METHOD

Before you get started, there are some salad jar rules you must follow. The rules of the LAYERS. It's important to make your salad in the right order to achieve ultimate freshness when it's time for the eating!

THE LAYERS ARE (FROM BOTTOM TO TOP):

1. Dressing (to avoid soggy salads, the dressing must always be the first layer at the bottom)
2. Moisture-resistant veggies
3. Protein
4. Grains, nuts, cheese
5. Leafy greens

When you're ready to eat, just unscrew the cap and shake into a bowl. No soggy salads here!

GREEK SALAD

Greek salad dressing (vinaigrette): 2 tablespoons olive oil, 1 tablespoon apple cider vinegar

Salt and pepper, to taste

Tomato chunks

Onion rings/chopped onion

Pitted olives

Cucumber

Feta cheese

Baby spinach

BURRITO JAR

Juice of half a lime

2 tablespoons olive oil

Salt and pepper, to taste

1 teaspoon dried cumin

Sour cream

Avocado

Beans

Corn

Quinoa

Tomatoes, chopped

Cheese

Cooked meat of your choice (optional)

Lettuce, chopped

OOBLECK
DIY

This DIY is for all you super-awesome science nerds, and, well, for anyone who loves SLIME! Guys, get ready, your mind is about to be BLOWN. Let me tell you about a little thing called OOBLECK. It is a **non-Newtonian** fluid—I'll pause here, because I know a lot of you are thinking, "EH?" This means it acts like a liquid when being poured, but acts like a solid when a force is acting on it. So, you can dip your hand slowly into it and it will act like a liquid, but if you squeeze the Oobleck or punch it, it will dry out and become more of a solid. I know, I know...AWESOME!

You may be wondering, "Oobleck...that's a pretty whacky name. I wonder what genius came up with that." Well, awesome people, it was the master of all rhymes and stories, Dr. Suess. He wrote a little tale called *Bartholomew and the Oobleck*. In the story, Oobleck, a gooey green substance, fell from the sky and wreaked havoc on the kingdom.

The best bit is, Oobleck is super easy to make. Here are some simple instructions for you.

INGREDIENTS

1 part water

1.5–2 parts cornstarch

A few drops of food coloring
(optional)

OOBLECK

- ✎ Pour the water in a bowl and add the cornstarch a little bit at a time. It's similar to making a basic icing recipe with icing sugar and water.
- ✎ Stir the mixture slowly until it has a gooey consistency. You may need to use your hands.
- ✎ When the Oobleck seems to be combined, slowly mix it while you add food coloring.

Now you can play with it!

SQUEEZE IT

PUNCH IT

PICK IT UP

POKE IT

It becomes solid when you apply pressure, however, when you stop moving it, the Oobleck will melt back into a liquid-like form. MIND BLOWN...right?

Is it a solid? Is it a liquid? Nah, man...

It's OOBLECK!

MAKE
TODAY
SO
AWESOME
yesterday
GETS
JEALOUS

QUICK... MAKE THE SILLIEST FACE EVER
AND STICK YOUR SELFIE HERE

#SELFIE

#SILLYFACESELFIE
#FEELAWESOME EVERY DAY

ELLY AWESOME'S WORDS OF WISDOM

There is no point worrying about things that are out of your control.

It is impossible to please everyone and for everyone to like you.

Don't be afraid to ask for help—we don't have all the answers and we're always learning!

Go with your gut—if something feels wrong or right, trust that feeling!

It's OK to make mistakes and fail—we learn and move on.

The mirror lies!

Be grateful and take notice of
the good things around you.

There is no such thing as a low-fat,
low-sugar brownie. Instagram is
lying to you!

Double deodorant does not equal
a shower. However, dry shampoo
totally equals a hair wash.

High heels are the worst. That is all.

Sunscreen was invented for
a reason. USE IT!

Anything can be breakfast.
There are no rules.

Tennis rackets don't double
as pasta strainers.

PLAN A DAY
WITH YOUR BESTIE

OK, so you've got a totes awesome date with your bestie. You've scrolled through your social media feeds enough and taken plenty of selfies and now you can't decide what to do next! I think it's time you made this AWESOME chatterbox to help you work it out!

Cut out the template opposite and follow these instructions:

1. FOLD YOUR TEMPLATE IN HALF AND THEN IN HALF AGAIN.

2. OPEN OUT, THEN TURN OVER SO THE TOP IS BLANK. FOLD EACH CORNER INTO THE MIDDLE.

3. TURN OVER AND REPEAT.

4. NOW, TURN OVER SO YOU CAN SEE THE PICTURES.

5. SLIDE YOUR THUMB AND INDEX FINGER BEHIND TWO OF THE PICTURES. PRESS TOGETHER.

6. REPEAT WITH THE THUMB AND INDEX FINGER OF YOUR OTHER HAND FOR THE OTHER TWO PICTURES.

7. ALL PICTURES SHOULD NOW BE AT THE FRONT WITH CENTERS TOUCHING.

TO PLAY...

With your thumbs and index fingers, move the chatterbox back and forth. Get your bestie to pick a number and open the flap to reveal an awesome activity.

1

MAKE STRESS BALLS

2

MAKE POPSICLES

8

MAKE A MUG CAKE

3

GO ON A SCAVENGER HUNT

DO THE PLAY DOUGH CHALLENGE

MOVIE MARATHON NIGHT! WHOO!

7

MAKE BFF PHONE CASES

MAKE AN AWESOME ANTHEMS PLAYLIST

6

4

5

cut ——————

fold ·············

105

BADASS BOOKWORM

I think books are pretty cool (obviously, duh, I've written one). Whether it's an ebook, audiobook, or the good old paperback, they are all just AWESOME. And here's why. They can make you laugh and make you cry. They can teach you things (e.g. how to feel awesome every day...high-five). They can keep you company when you feel lonely and they can take you to worlds you never knew existed. I could go on, but I think you've got it...

So, awesome people, what are your five all-time fave books? OR what five books have you got on your awesome must-read list?

SHARE YOUR FAVES #FEELAWESOMEEVERYDAY

OBVI THIS IS ONE OF YOUR FAVES!

HOW TO FEEL AWESOME EVERY DAY

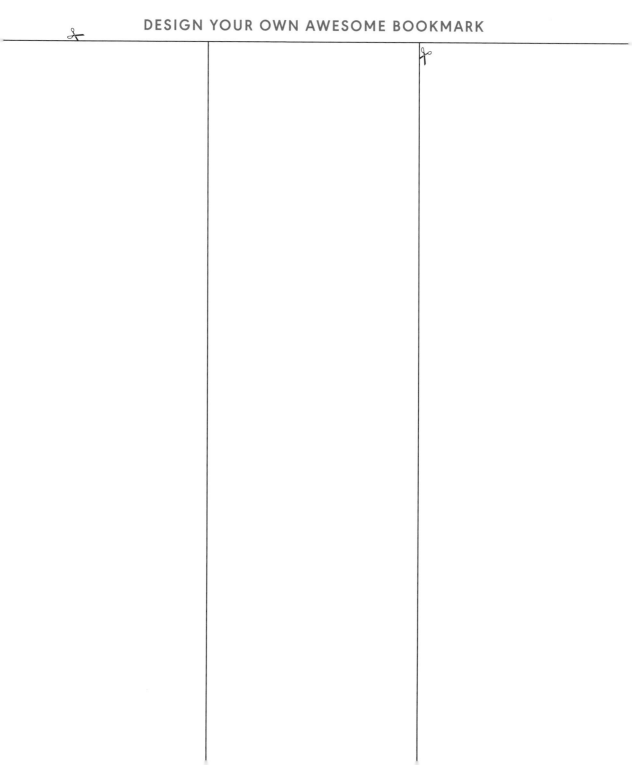

You have one whole hour of uninterrupted ME TIME—WOOP!

List ten AWESOME things you plan on doing...

1. _____

2. _____

3. _____

4. _____

5. _____

6. _____

7. _____

8. _____

9. _____

10. _____

Awesome text alert

Tell the people you love how much they mean to you right now.

MINI THANK-YOU CARDS

Isn't it awesome when you receive an unexpected thank-you note? Here are a few ready-to-go mini thank-you cards to cut out, write in and hand out!

COME GET YA COUPONS!

Who doesn't love a coupon? Especially the ones you can exchange for free pizza! Anyway, enough about pizza, I'm getting hungry... These super-cool friend coupons are totally awesome! Cut them up and share them with all your besties.

Fill in the blank ones with more awesome things you can do with your BFFs.

AWESOME ENDS WITH ... ME

WINTER BUCKET LIST

Get out your cute pajamas, fluffy socks, cozy throws and snuggle on down...WINTER IS COMING!

CHECK LIST

- ○ Go to an art gallery
- ○ Write a short story
- ○ Go stargazing
- ○ Have a cozy breakfast in bed
- ○ Try a new sport
- ○ Redecorate your room

○ Cook something you've never cooked before

○ Start a book club

○ Netflix binge (those series won't watch themselves)

○ Make some trading cards

○ Play tourist in your own city

○ Throw a board game party!

○ Plan a mega movie marathon night

○ Bake festive cookies

○ Host a karaoke party

pretty awesome pinwheels

On the menu today we have oven-roasted spiral pastry rolls, layered with tomato puree, creamy cheese and tender bits of smoked ham...a.k.a. pinwheels. OK, I was trying to make it sound fancy, but at the end of the day, it's a super-tasty snack you should totally try. Growing up, this recipe was one of my absolute favorites. My mum used to make them with me and my sister all the time!

They are so easy and seriously YUM, I'm going to have to make one right now!

INGREDIENTS

3 sheets puff pastry, defrosted

4 tablespoons pizza sauce (or ketchup, tomato sauce, or barbecue sauce)

1 cup grated cheese

½ cup ham or bacon, chopped

PRETTY AWESOME PINWHEELS

- Preheat your oven to 350°F (or 180°C).
- Defrost your puff pastry sheets. Don't worry about defrosting completely — they just need to be soft enough to roll.
- Spread the sauce over each piece of puff pastry (just on the side facing up).
- Sprinkle the ham and cheese over the pastry.
- Roll each pastry sheet up into a log shape. Cut into discs or pinwheels.
- Lay the pinwheels on a baking tray lined with baking paper.
- Bake for about 20 minutes or to the instructed time on your pastry box. The pinwheels will be ready when the pastry is puffy and golden.

SERVE AND DEVOUR!

MAKES 12

DOTS AND BOXES GAME

This game is amazing! It can be played almost anywhere and makes people of all ages get sooooo competitive. The aim of the game... try to make more boxes than your opponent! It will have you tapping your pens and racking your brain for ways to win!

So, how do we play this awesome game? It's super simple.

A player's turn consists of connecting two horizontally or vertically adjacent dots with a line (to make a square, ya follow?). Dots must be next to each other and diagonal lines aren't allowed.

A point is scored each time a player completes a square. When a square is created, the turn stays with the player who made the square, otherwise the turns alternate.

Use two different colored pens when you play, otherwise things will get pretty confusing!

Write your initials in the boxes you complete. Then you can count who made the most boxes at the end.

BIG DAY COUNTDOWN

Looking forward to a big event, special occasion, or important milestone always gets me feeling pretty awesome. Think about something you are REALLY excited about and let's start a COUNTDOWN!

I CAN'T WAIT FOR

_____

YEARS
_____

MONTHS
_____

WEEKS
_____

DAYS
_____

HOURS
_____

MINUTES
_____

THE OPTIMIST SEES THE DOUGHNUT, THE PESSIMIST THE HOLE!

Oscar Wilde

DECORATE THIS
DOUGHNUT ↓

AND
THIS
ONE!

Elly Awesome's signature Guacamole

I LOVE guacamooooollllleeeee!
I can't get enough of it. It's good on
its own, and on top of tacos, inside
burritos, resting on ya nachos....
Let's face it, it's the best and this is
my signature guac recipe!

INGREDIENTS

2 avocados, mashed

¼ red onion, finely chopped

2 teaspoons lemon juice

1 teaspoon smoked paprika

1 small tomato, chopped

2 tablespoons sour cream

salt and pepper, to taste

ELLY AWESOME'S SIGNATURE GUACAMOLE

Mash the avocados in a bowl and then stir in the remaining ingredients.

SIMPLE.

*

AWESOME TIP ALERT
THIS GUACAMOLE
IS OMG YUM
ON NACHOS.

*

NACHOS

Here's what to do...

Cover a plate with tortilla chips. Add beans, corn, chopped tomato, cooked chicken, and salsa. Sprinkle grated cheese on top. Put in the microwave on high for about a minute. Once the cheese is melted to your liking, add the fresh guacamole on top and CHOW DOWN!

PLAN THE ULTIMATE MOVIE NIGHT

Write your favorite movies on the tickets below. Then cut them out, put them in a hat or jar and pick one out when you can't decide which movie to watch.

CUT OUT THESE TICKETS

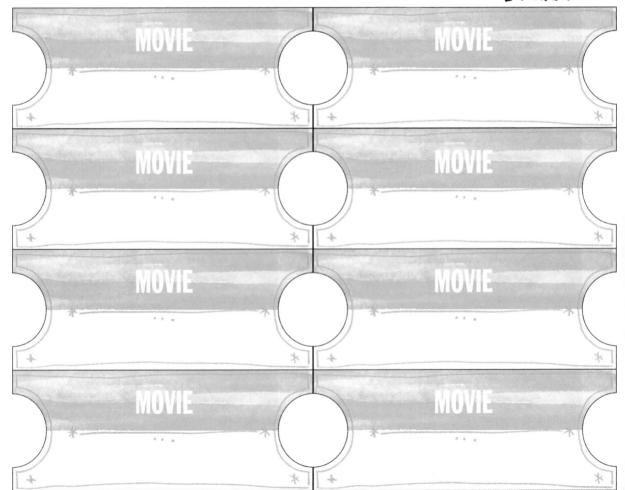

MOVIE . . .   MOVIE . . .

MOVIE . . .   MOVIE . . .

MOVIE . . .   MOVIE . . .

MOVIE . . .   MOVIE . . .

It's time to settle in and watch some movies with your friends! Get organizing with my awesome planner for the ultimate night in.

GUEST LIST

YOUR GUESTS NEED TO BRING...

TASTY SNACKS: SAVOURY

WHAT ARE WE DRINKING?

TASTY SNACKS: SWEET

DRESS CODE (PJS OBVS.)

TABLET CASE
DIY

Awesome people, you do NOT need to spend heaps of money on your new tablet or phone case! In fact, you can make your own CUSTOM phone case for about $5! Be the envy of all your mates with these two totally awesome DIY designs.

SIMPLY AWESOME CASE

1. First, find some wrapping paper, a comic book or something with a cool pattern.

YOU WILL NEED
- ★ Your tablet/phone
- ★ Wrapping paper/ comic book/paper with an awesome pattern
- ★ A transparent case for your device

2. Trace around your device case on your chosen paper with a pen or pencil.

3. Cut out the tracing and lay it into the back of your transparent device case, with the pattern facing outwards. If it doesn't quite fit, you may need to trim the edges (little by little) until it does.

4. Put the case on your device and BAM you've got yourself a custom case that you can change any time!

BFF CASE

1. Draw a heart (or use a stencil) onto the colored laminate with a pen. Make sure the heart is big enough to fit over two devices. Look at your phone or tablet to determine how big the heart should be.

2. Very neatly, cut out the heart shape.

3. Now, cut the heart as best as you can down the middle.

4. Stick half of the heart on your phone and the other half on your BFF's.

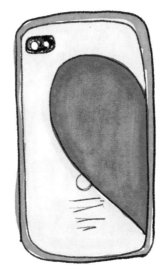
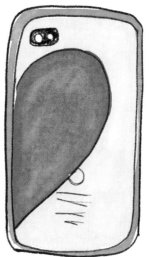

AWESOME EMOJI
dictionary

 THIS IS AWESOME, AMAZING, FANTASTIC NEWS!

 LET'S HANG THIS WEEKEND AND HAVE A SUPER-AWESOME TIME.

 EXTREME EMBARRASSMENT NARROWLY AVOIDED... PHEW!

 WHAT DO YOU MEAN THERE'S NO ICE CREAM LEFT?!

 YOU ARE GIVING ME SERIOUS LOLS. I TOTALLY NEARLY PEED.

 I MAY HAVE EATEN ALL THE PIZZA. I REALLY HOPE NO ONE FINDS OUT.

 SO, I DON'T HAVE THE GUTS TO SAY IT, BUT I THINK YOU'RE PRETTY CUTE!

 WHATEVER THAT SMELL IS... IT WASN'T ME.

 INTERNATIONAL RESPONSE TO PUPPY/KITTEN PHOTO.

 MOST AWESOME EMOJI OUT THERE WITH MULTIPLE DEFINITIONS.

 WHY IS MY WIFI NOT WORKING?

 YOU HAVE ANGERED ME WITH YOUR VERY UN-AWESOME BEHAVIOUR.

OH MAN, I'M SO GROSSED OUT RIGHT NOW. GONNA BARF.

 I AM SHOWING EXCITED APPRECIATION FOR ALL THE FOOD I AM ABOUT TO EAT.

 I DEFINITELY JUST SAW THE BIGGEST HAIRY SPIDER! YOU GOTTA COME HELP ME!

 TOO MANY FEELS, I CAN'T EVEN!

 YEP, I'M AWESOME.

ADD TO THE AWESOME EMOJI DICTIONARY AND DRAW YOUR FAVES BELOW WITH A LITTLE DEFINITION!

 I'M FEELING MISCHIEVOUS. LET'S MAKE A PLAN!

 HIGH-FIVE, AWESOME PERSON.

 ALL HAIL THE WEEKEND/PIZZA/ PUPPIES/KITTENS.

Fruit Wands

So, awesome people, you may not know this about me... I LOVE FRUIT. I can't get enough of the stuff, which is why I had to include these super-awesome FRUIT WANDS. They're so simple and totally YUM, and let's face it, they look pretty cool! You can load your wands up with as much fruit as it can handle—there are no rules with these bad boys!

INGREDIENTS

FRUIT!!! Use any of your favorite fruits. I always use watermelon, kiwi, strawberries, grapes, and melon.

YOU WILL NEED

Small cookie cutters

A knife

Skewers

FRUIT WANDS

- ✐ Wash the fruit and then cut into pieces thick enough (approx. 1 in.) to put onto a skewer.
- ✐ Use cookie cutters on the harder fruits, such as melons, to cut super-cool shapes.
- ✐ Push all your fruit onto the skewers and serve!

PHONE SPEAKER
DIY

If I told you that a cardboard toilet roll tube could be used as a phone speaker, would you think I've gone mad? Guess what? I'm telling you that a cardboard toilet paper tube CAN be used as a phone speaker and it works quite well! Who doesn't love a good DIY life hack?!

YOU WILL NEED

Cardboard tube

Washi tape or patterned paper, for decoration

Pencil

Thumbtacks

Scissors

Small blob of clay

1. Stand your phone on top of the cardboard tube and work out where to make the cuts so your phone can sit inside it.

2. Draw around the bottom of your phone onto the cardboard.

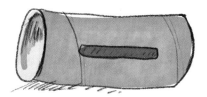

3. Using scissors or a sharp knife, cut the cardboard carefully. You want a snug fit for your phone inside the tube to improve the sound.

4. Now it's time to decorate the tube. I used washi tape as it is super easy to use and comes in loads of cool patterns.

5. Use 2 or 4 thumbtacks, pushed into the underside of the cardboard tube to help the "speaker" stand up.

6. Mold clay around pointed tips or add bits of rubber erasers to create a non-slip grip. This will also help to keep thumbtacks from scratching surfaces.

7. Insert phone into your awesome new speaker and press play!

I AM NOT
AFRAID OF
TOMORROW
for I have
SEEN
yesterday
AND I
LOVE
TODAY

WILLIAM
ALLEN
WHITE

COLOR OVER YOUR FEAR UNTIL IT'S NO MORE
THEN SCRIBBLE ALL OVER THIS PAGE!

CRAZY CUISINE

I have sampled heaps of weird and wonderful food from around the world. Some I fell in love with, some I wasn't quite sure of, and some (sorry, there is no delicate way to put this) made me want to throw up. My tastebuds have been through it all, so now I'm spreading the word to you fine people, and hopefully you'll want to try out more crazy cuisines from around the world. No matter what the food tastes like, it's awesome to try out new foods and learn a bit about the country it comes from. So, here is a little selection of the good, the bad, and the ugly. You should give them a go!

*
AWESOME TIP ALERT
BEST WAY TO WARM THESE BAD BOYS UP IS TO BALANCE THEM ON TOP OF YOUR HOT MUG OF TEA OR COFFEE.
NOM NOM NOM.
*

THE DISH

Stroopwafels

THE COUNTRY

The Netherlands

WHAT IS IT?

The best waffles you'll ever eat

THE VERDICT

These gooey waffles will blow your mind. They have a layer of syrup inside and they are chewy and squishy when warmed up.
Best texture ever.

THE DISH

Green Tea Mochi Ice Cream

THE COUNTRY

Japan

WHAT IS IT?

Green tea–flavored ice cream with a soft and smooshy rice coating

THE VERDICT

What an AWESOME combo, Japan, I salute you! The rice coating gives the ice cream an amazing texture. I love the refreshing and delicious flavor green tea has when it's mixed with ice cream.

THE DISH

Palak Paneer

THE COUNTRY

India

WHAT IS IT?

Spinach curry with cheese

THE VERDICT

The old saying "never judge a book by its cover" must be applied when it comes to this dish. I'll admit, when I was faced with a bowl full of green mush, my first thought was... NAH! It looked so gross, I almost turned my nose up at this creamy spinach and cheese curry. However, awesome people, that green mush is DEEEEELICIOUS! The taste is UNREAL.

THE DISH

Poutine

THE COUNTRY

Canada

WHAT IS IT?

French fries topped with cheese curds and gravy

THE VERDICT

Bravo, Canada, bravo. A sensational way to jazz up some fries.

THE DISH

Churrasco (a.k.a. Brazilian barbecue)

THE COUNTRY

Brazil

WHAT IS IT?

All the grilled meats

THE VERDICT

An amazing dine-in experience where you get all-you-can-eat meat until you're full. When you go to a Brazilian barbecue restaurant, the waiters will come over to you every five minutes with giant skewers of different kinds of meat to offer you. There are so many options and they often serve a delicious cheesy bread called *Pão de Queijo*. Super YUM, but sorry all you veggies, this one is not for you!

THE DISH

Durian

THE COUNTRY

Indonesia and Malaysia

WHAT IS IT?

A large spikey fruit

THE VERDICT

So, word on the street is this fruit is pretty popular in Malaysia. I can't quite understand why because it smells and tastes like a fart. To some people, this bizarre fruit is yumdidlyumptious, but it is just way too much for my tastebuds!

THE DISH

Fried Polenta

THE COUNTRY

Italy

WHAT IS IT?

Boiled cornmeal. Once it has cooled and solidified it can be baked, fried, or grilled

THE VERDICT

YUM! It is chewy and crunchy on the outside while the inside stays soft and creamy. Try dipping in your favorite sauces... DELIZIOSO!

EAT.
SLEEP.
BE AWESOME.
—REPEAT—

AWESOME PEOPLE, I CHALLENGE YOU TO DESIGN
THE MOST AWESOME T-SHIRT EVER!

#FEELAWESOMEEVERYDAY

playdough

DIY

Oh, playdough. The memories. Sure, it seems like a kid thing but anyone can enjoy playing with it! In fact, loads of people have been taking part in the "playdough challenge." The rules of the challenge are, you and a friend compete against each other to make random things from playdough within a twenty-second time limit. Get another friend to judge the competition and call out weird and wonderful things for you to make. So, if you get told to make a dog, you and your friend have twenty seconds to complete your playdough masterpiece. Whoever makes the best one in the time frame wins. Usually, all the creations look ridiculous, but that's why people play it—'cause it is hilarious!

This challenge can get pretty intense, believe me! So why not stock up your playdough supplies and make your own...?

INGREDIENTS

1 cup plain flour

3 heaping tablespoons salt

½ cup water

1 to 2 tablespoons cooking oil

A few drops food coloring
  (optional)

PLAYDOUGH

↗ Mix the flour and salt together in a
  large mixing bowl. Then add the water
  and oil.

↗ Knead until the mixture becomes
  smooth. This may take 5–10 minutes.

↗ As you knead the dough, you might
  have to add more flour or water to get
  the consistency smooth rather than
  sticky.

↗ If you want to color your playdough,
  add food coloring and knead until the
  color is fully blended in.

Your playdough can be stored in a plastic
bag in the fridge.

DRAW YOUR FAVORITE TOPPINGS ON THE PIZZA SLICE

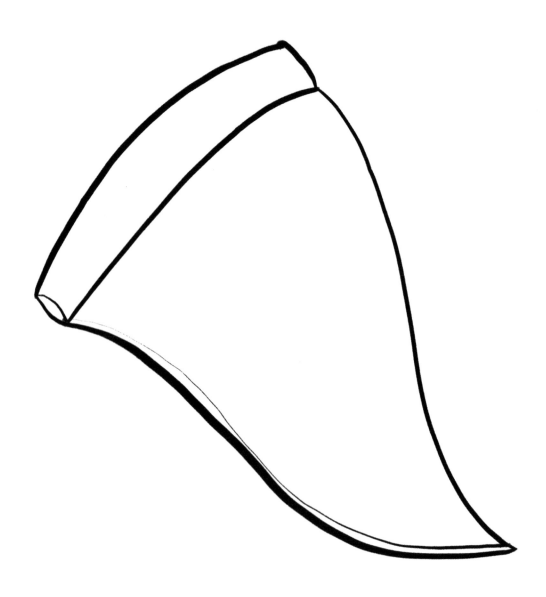

GOOD

F🍩🍔D

GOOD
MOOD

SQUISHY STRESS BALL DIY

*
AWESOME TIP ALERT
IT'S BEST TO MAKE
THESE OUTSIDE AS
IT COULD
GET MESSY!
*

A big part of feeling awesome is being able to get rid of any stress or worry that might be weighing you down. Anxiety and stress ain't no joke, bro. So, if you're racking your brains over your impossible homework or working out how to deal with some worrying news, then SQUEEZE, SQUISH, AND SQUASH the stress away with this awesome homemade stress ball.

YOU WILL NEED

★ Party balloons

★ Flour for the filling (or you could try playdough, rice or sand)

★ Funnel

★ Scissors

1. Blow up a balloon to stretch it. Then let out the air.

2. Use the funnel to fill up the balloon with your filling of choice. Hold the end of the balloon around the funnel tightly to avoid spilling. If you're struggling to get the filling into the balloon with the funnel, use a pen to encourage the flow.

3. Fill the balloon so it's almost full, but DO NOT fill up the neck.

4. Then, without losing too much of the filling, gently and slowly massage the balloon a bit to release any excess air inside it. Carefully cut off the neck of the balloon (yes, there will be a big open hole on the top of your stress ball).

5. Now for the tricky part. Get another balloon, cut off the neck and then stretch it over your stress ball so it completely encapsulates it. This should seal the stress ball.

6. Add a third balloon the same way to make sure the stress ball is extra sealed.

7. If you want to add a bit of decoration to your stress ball, take a different colored balloon, cut off the neck, fold it in half and cut out different shapes on the side and stretch it over the stress ball.

HOW TO GET RID OF A BAD MOOD

I'm going to let you in on a secret. I, Elly Awesome, have been in some pretty bad moods in my time. I'm talking black, rumbling clouds of grumpy. I know, right? Shock horror! But we all have our off days, and let me tell you, it's OK. The trick is knowing how to work through the bad mood and getting back to feeling tip-top. Hey, I never said this awesome malarkey was easy— sometimes you gotta work at it.

So, let's start at the beginning and work through your moody funk.

HOW DO YOU LOOK WHEN YOU'RE IN A BAD MOOD?

How do you act when you're in a bad mood?

_____

_____

How do the people around you act when you're in a bad mood?

_____

_____

_____

What are some ways to cope with a bad mood? I'll start you off, then you think of some more...

· Call a friend
· Squeeze a stress ball

_____
_____
_____

You should be feeling a bit more positive now. Think about what fueled your bad mood. Circle your emotion.

Sadness   Fear   Frustration

Guilt   Embarrassment   Worry

Disappointment   Jealousy   Anger

Shame

OK, you've established how to cope with your mood, now let's list some ways to fight the funk and get rid of this grump once and for all.
Fill in the positive things and memories you associate with the below.

Two things you can smell

_____

Two things you can hear

_____

Two things you can feel

_____

Two things you can see

_____

Two things you can eat

_____

Have you learned anything from how you feel when you're in a bad mood?

_____
_____
_____
_____
_____

Can you take anything positive from this bad mood?

_____
_____
_____
_____
_____

AWESOME ANTHEMS

The one thing—apart from puppies...oh and pizza—that is guaranteed to make me feel awesome is MUSIC! So, awesome person, compile a soundtrack full of all your fave anthems!

1 _____

2 _____

3 _____

4 _____

5 _____

6 _____

7 _____

8 _____

9 _____

10 _____

11 _____

12 _____

13 _____

14 _____

Now create your AWESOME ANTHEMS cover art here!

Who do you want to listen to this mix with?

_____

Oreo cheesecake bites

Who loves cheesecake and who loves Oreos?! I don't know about you but I'm flailing my hands around in the air yelling "ME!!!" They are two of my FAVORITE things and this recipe brings the two together. It's glorious! And, oh snap, it's another amazing quick and easy recipe thanks to ya gal, Elly Awesome. I know you will LOVE these, so grab the ingredients and give it a go!

INGREDIENTS

20 Oreos

½ cup cream cheese

⅔ cup icing sugar

OREO CHEESECAKE BITES

- Blend the Oreos in a food processor until they are nice and crumbly.

- Using a mixer (if you don't have a mixer, the old wooden spoon and muscle power will have to do!), combine the cream cheese, Oreo crumbles, and sugar.

- Use a small ice-cream scoop to make bite-sized balls. Or scoop a spoonfull and roll into shape with your hands.

- Place each bite into small cupcake pans and put in the freezer for 2 hours.

SERVE AND ENJOY! WOO HOO!

MAKES APPROX. 20 BALLS

Do you have a favorite quote or
inspirational saying that makes you
feel AWESOME?

Write it down on the opposite page
and then decorate around it.

You can even cut the page out
and display your super awesome
amazing artwork on the wall!

LOOK UP
AT THE NIGHT SKY

Staring at the stars in the sky is one of my fave things to do. It chills me out and gets me thinking about anything and everything. How many of you are just totally in awe of the universe we live in? Yeah, me too. We are just a tiny speck in this humongous cosmos. Mind-blowing and yet completely AWESOME!

To fully appreciate your place on this planet (and take a little time to think about any alien buddies out there), get outside and do some stargazing.

This is the perfect opportunity to be still, be mindful of your breathing, relax, and take in that starry sky.

*
AWESOME ALERT
SEE IF YOU CAN SPOT ANY CONSTELLATIONS. IF YOU HAVE FRIENDS IN THE OTHER HEMISPHERE, THEY WILL SEE DIFFERENT CONSTELLATIONS! A-MAZING!
*

AWESOME NIGHTTIME STRETCHES

Getting those all-important Zzzzzzzzzzzs is essential for awesomeness every day. Sometimes, though, it's hard to switch off from a stressful day and you end up lying in bed, wide awake. Grrrrrrrrrr. So, awesome people, if you want to clear your mind and slip into a peaceful slumber, try out these simple stretches. The best thing is that you can do them in bed! Hold each stretch for one minute—you'll be snoring in no time.

LEGS-UP-THE-WALL RELAXATION

Lie back on your bed and extend your legs up the wall.

WIND-DOWN TWIST

Sit up and cross your legs. Place your right hand on your left knee and place your left hand behind you. Exhale and gently twist your body to the left. Breathe deeply and then return to center. Repeat on the opposite side.

SUPER-AWESOME STRETCH

Lie on your back with your knees bent. Place your feet together and let your knees fall open. Let your arms rest by your side and breathe deeply. (You may fall asleep at this point. I don't call it the Super-Awesome Stretch for nothing.)

KNEE HUGS

Hug your knees to your chest, cross your ankles and wrap your arms around your shins. Breathe in and rock your body up to sit. As you roll back, breathe out. Continue this for one minute, then stretch, get super comfy, and Zzzzzzzzzzzzzzzzzzzzzzzzzz.

I'M IN LOVE
with my bed,
BUT MY ALARM CLOCK
won't let us
BE TOGETHER

COLOR IN THE SQUARES

COLORING SQUARES AND CREATING COOL PATTERNS CAN BE VERY RELAXING. TRUST ME!

Sweet dreams Dreamcatcher

During the hours we are awake, we try to keep our awesome levels as high as possible, am I right? This got me thinking, what about at night? Is there a way we can keep our dream world awesome too? Well, awesome people, let me tell you about the DREAMCATCHER. Native American legends say that the cool spider-web design inside a dreamcatcher allows all the good dreams to pass through and float down the hanging beads and feathers to you, sleeping below in your bed. Pretty cool, huh? The best bit about this nifty design is, when a bad dream comes floating along, it gets stuck in the web! No more bad dreams, WOO HOO! I'm all for happy dreams, so how about we make one?!

This project is a bit fiddly, but be patient, it's totally worth it.

YOU WILL NEED

★ Embroidery hoop (alternatively, if you want to make a mini dreamcatcher, a bangle is perfect!)

★ Scissors

★ String (colored or plain)

★ Feathers

★ Beads

★ Ribbon and lace for additional decoration (optional)

1. Tie your string in a knot around the hoop and then wrap it around until the whole hoop is completely covered. Tie a double knot at the end to make a hanging loop and cut off the remaining thread.

2. Now comes the fiddly part—the SPIDER WEB. The traditional spider-web design is pretty tricky to accomplish, so I have opted for a slightly simpler approach. Secure your string at Point 1 on the hoop with a knot. Stretch the string to Point 2 and wrap around the hoop a few times to secure. Then, stretch the string to Point 3 and secure, then to Point 4 and so on until you are back to where you started at Point 1. Pull the string tight and secure with a knot.

3. Take a feather and tie one end to a piece of string. Once you have secured the feather at the bottom of the string, thread on an assortment of beads.

4. Tie the string to the bottom of the hoop. Repeat step 3 to make more dangling feathers and attach to the bottom of the hoop.

5. If you want to add more decorations, tie on some ribbon and lace between the dangling feathers.

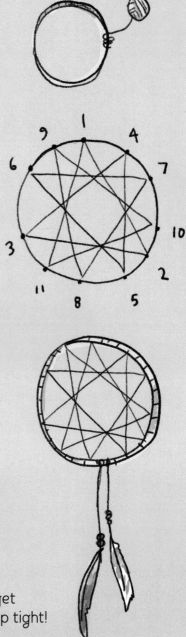

Hang your dreamcatcher above your bed and get ready for some truly AWESOME dreams! Sleep tight!

ABOUT MY DREAMS

Isn't it weird how dreams can sometimes be really hard to remember? Quick, scribble down what your last dream was about so you don't forget!

CHECKERS!

What can I say? Checkers is a classic!
It's practically been around since the time o' Jurassic.
I used to play this with my family growing up.
Once you learn how to play it's really hard to stop!
You can play it on the dining table, on a road trip
or on your couch.

It's a simple game for everyone and fun for even a grouch!

Instructions

Checkers is a board game played between two players who alternate moves. Each player has twelve pieces placed on the twelve dark squares closest to their edge of the board. The player who can no longer make any moves—because they have no more pieces or because all their pieces are blocked—loses the game.

MOVING

A piece that is not a king can move one square, diagonally forward. A king can move diagonally, forward or backward. Any piece (piece or king) can only move to a vacant square. A move can also consist of one or more jumps.

JUMPING

If one of your opponent's checkers is on a forward diagonal next to one of your checkers, and the next space diagonally beyond the opponent's checker is empty, then your checker must jump the opponent's checker and land in the space beyond. Your opponent's checker is captured and removed from the board.

 After making one jump, your checker might have another jump available from its new position. Your checker must take that jump too. It must continue to jump until there are no more jumps available. Both pieces and kings are allowed to make multiple jumps.

KINGING

When one of your checkers reaches the opposite side of the board, it is crowned and becomes a king. You can "crown" your kinged piece either by flipping the piece over if there is an image (usually a crown) printed on the the flip side, or by placing a captured piece on top of the kinged piece, to distinguish it from other pieces. Your turn ends there.

 A king can move backward as well as forward along the diagonals. It still can only move a distance of one space at a time. It must still jump when possible, and it must take all jumps that are available to it. In each jump, the king can only jump over one opposing piece at a time, and it must land in the space just beyond the captured piece. The king cannot move multiple spaces before or after jumping a piece.

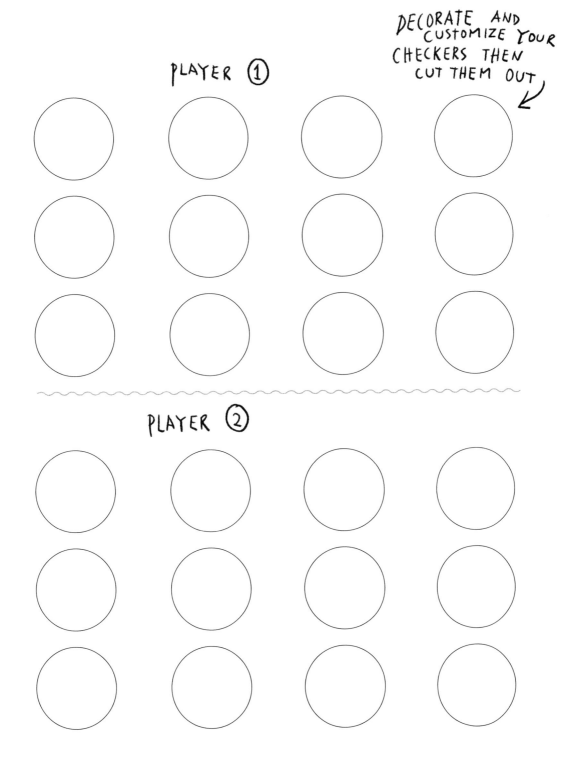

PLAY CHECKERS HERE!

STEP-BY-STEP GUIDE TO MAKING AN AWESOME VIDEO

Everyone has different reasons for starting a YouTube channel or vlog. Me? I was all about spreading the joy of all things awesome (obvs). Whatever your reason, here are some of my SWEET tips to help you make an AWESOME video!

THE IDEA

First, think of an idea! What do people want to watch? What do you want to watch? It's always a good idea to make a video about something you're passionate about. You could make a video teaching people how to do something, telling people how to solve a problem, or you could review a product. You could even make a comedy sketch or play some video games or apps for people's entertainment! There are so many things you can do. Once you think of your idea, write down a few bullet points of what you want to say or show in your video. You could even go one step further and write a whole script for your video.

THE GEAR

Camera

You'll need some kind of camera. These days your phone or tablet can totally do the trick and I would highly recommend using these when you are starting out. However, if you want to step things up a notch and make your vids look more profesh, I would recommend getting a camera with a flip-up screen. If you want to vlog, the flip-up screen makes it easier to set up shots when you film yourself. Most of the professional YouTubers and vloggers use DSLR cameras with interchangeable lenses. The awesome thing about these cameras is you can buy different lenses to change how the video looks. Also, if you invest in a decent one, you won't need to upgrade your camera for many years—you can just buy different lenses to change things up. **Do bear in mind**, these cameras aren't cheap! If you want to take the plunge and invest, make sure you do your research so you know what you're buying.

Lights

It's really important to have as much lighting as possible for your video. The best thing to do is make use of all the natural light available to you. My advice would be to set up your filming spot right in front of a window. The better lit you are, the more professional your video will look. Also, good lighting can make footage from lower quality cameras look way more impressive. If the natural light where you are filming isn't that great, turn on every light in the room, grab a few extra lamps to angle at your face and light up the shot. If you want your videos to look super slick, you could invest in some soft box lights or some LED light panels.

Microphone

Clear sound is essential when making a video. People might forgive you for having low-quality video footage, but if it's hard to hear what you're saying or the sound is unclear, they are unlikely to stick around and watch. So, I highly recommend using a microphone. If you don't own/can't afford a standalone microphone or a microphone that plugs into your camera, there are a few things you can do to make your videos sound the best they possibly can:

☺ Shoot your video in a quiet place.

☺ Avoid filming in large rooms that might have an echo.

☺ Place the camera closer to your face rather than farther away.

Tripod

You don't want to make your viewers feel seasick with a shaky video! To avoid this and make the video more professional, I use a tripod to hold the camera steady. However, it is not essential to have a tripod when creating your awesome videos, just do whatever you can to stand your phone/tablet/camera up in front of you. Universal tablet/phone stands are pretty good, or you can simply prop up your camera with a stack of books. Alternatively, if you just want to vlog, you could use a selfie stick for a unique angle.

Memory cards

I would suggest investing in a memory card that has a larger capacity—even if it costs more money. The last thing you want is to be filming for a while but then discover the camera has stopped recording because the card is full. Avoiding this frustration is worth it, and if you find you don't film THAT much, you might not even need to spend money buying a second one.

Backup hard drive

If you're really serious about making videos, you may want to invest in a backup hard drive. I always save my video footage and finished videos to my backup hard drive in case something were to happen to them. Also, it's cool to keep a lot of your raw footage to come back to and look at or use as content for future videos.

Headphones

OK, so it's not totally necessary, but I like to edit my videos wearing headphones. This helps me hear all the sounds in my video clearly and to experience what it would be like for viewers to hear the video (as many people wear headphones while watching). You may want to invest in some comfy over-ear headphones.

THE EDITING

You can edit your video on pretty much any program—whatever you can get your hands on or whatever works for you. For example, there's Sony Vegas, Adobe Premiere, Final Cut Pro X, iMovie, Windows Movie Maker... I started out with iMovie because it was free and it worked really well for me. I'd recommend starting out with a free program and then working your way up. To learn how to edit, I just watched tons of YouTube tutorials on how to use particular editing programs. You get better the more you create videos and practice. Once you become proficient at editing, you can download the more expensive editing programs and give their free trials a go. Then, once you get the hang of editing, you could consider purchasing them. Often, the paid programs have more features, but you may not need them unless you want to get really fancy with your edits! So, give them a try before whipping out the credit card!

And finally . . . THE SHARING

Once you've edited your video, it's all about getting it out there and having it seen by the people of the world. Use captivating titles that spark curiosity or emotion and create a colorful thumbnail for your video. If you're wondering how to get clicks, next time you're scrolling around on the internet looking for a video to watch, think about what usually catches your eye. What made you click on the last video you watched? Really think about this for the next videos you check out and try to work out how you can apply that to your videos.

You can also share your videos on social media and forums that relate to your video content.

One last thing . . . THE TROLLS

Sadly, awesome people, I have to mention the trolls. Once in a while, every YouTuber will receive a negative or unpleasant comment. PLEASE REMEMBER, this is not a reflection of your hard work! Stay confident about the AWESOME content you have created and stay focused on the positive comments you receive. Most importantly, DO NOT FEED THE TROLLS!!! Ignore the negativity and just interact with your supporters and fans!

STAY AWESOME. FEEL AWESOME. BE AWESOME.

MAKE YOUR OWN AWESOME
MOMENTS COLLAGE

#FEELAWESOMEEVERYDAY

CONGRATULATIONS

You have finally come to the end of your awesome journey and I am proud to present you with your ADVANCED DIPLOMA OF AWESOME.
Now, awesome person, it is up to you to spread the knowledge you have learned here and help the world FEEL. AWESOME. EVERY. DAY.

ADVANCED   DIPLOMA   OF

Awesome

PRESENTED   TO

SIGNED BY

Elly Awesome

GO FORTH AND BE AWESOME